Reinvent Yourself

Reinvent Yourself

MAKAYLA PHOMPHACHANH

To order additional copies of this book, contact:
Xlibris
1-888-795-4274
www.Xlibris.com
Orders@Xlibris.com
812544

Contents

It is with great pleasure that I welcome you into a journey of heartbreak, betrayal, remorse, intimacy and growth. First and foremost, thank you so much for purchasing my poem book. I am extremely grateful for the support. I created this book as a way to escape from my emotions towards the many obstacles that I have faced, and even the ones that am currently facing. My purpose in writing this book is to highlight the fact that people all go through similar feelings. Everyone goes through something, so if you have been hurt or are currently hurting just know that you are not alone. Always remember that aligning with your true authentic self is so important. Things fall apart to make way for something new to enter. You might not understand your current obstacles but you will eventually. All things align for a greater good. You just need to have faith that things will always improve. Appreciate the hard journey because it made you stronger, wiser and braver. Let go of anything holding you back from achieving happiness. I hope you enjoy these poems, it was made with an abundance of emotions.

- MK

Rest

Reset

Release

Redefine

Realign

You'll come out this cocoon a butterfly.

Mishandled:

Heart has been misused

Starting to feel abused

My feelings are confused

It's giving me the blues

Betrayal:

I have my guard up high

My trust does nothing but sigh

I try to see things with an open eye

But it's hard when all I'm use to is lies

Broken:

Heart is scarred

I'm trying to get it up to par

But it's hard

People always catch me off guard

Humble:

Tryna find a hustle

Put together the puzzle

Get myself out this bubble

At times I can stumble

But I never fully fumble

Hard times make me snuffle

But I'll get through this struggle

As long as I always remain humble

Help:

Heart is weary

Eyes are teary

I'm feeling eerie

Who will cure me?

Absence:

Growing up I never had a father figure

Makes me feel bitter

And causes some triggers

The word "dad" is so unfamiliar

Make it make sense:

I always accuse you

Of things that I would do

My guilt is what makes my heart break into two

I'm sorry for the way I keep doing you boo

Urgency:

Why do you keep hurting me

My feelings are starting to burden me

Your emotions are so obscure to me

The love is starting to worry me

Truth to be told:

We're only getting older

And my heart is just getting colder

All this pain is turning me into a soldier

True colors:

Made mistakes

Some put my life at sake

Made me cry up a lake

But it revealed the fake

Isolation:

Fell in love with my solitude

It brings a lot of volume

For me to conclude

That it's bad to let people intrude

I don't care how I'm viewed

Because I'm at a higher altitude

Than the people from my past that I surpassed

Cancelled:

Heart is broke

So I'm always woke

My love is revoked

Because I get treated like a joke

November 24, 1979:

My mom is strong

She hasn't cried in so long

She always says nothing is wrong

But I know her feelings have been prolonged

Separation:

I say I'm okay

I'm always being betrayed

But I forgive and continue moving up the stairway

I take it day by day

Cloak:

This feeling of lust

It's messing up my trust

You treat me like dust

Leaving me with a feeling of disgust

Row the boat:

Been going through some things that I never show

Shed a few tears but you'll never know

Crazy that all these things happened years ago

But for some reason I'm still feeling low

Remember me:

Will you remember me

The way you felt laying next to me

How I made you feel so free

What happened to you and me

Come and see me:

I miss your kisses

Now all we have are burnt bridges

Can you come visit

Our relationship was so explicit

Winning your heart back is my only mission

Detain:

Hard to let go of the past

The joy you brought me was vast

Your love showed a contrast

Our connection is unsurpassed

August 6, 2017:

I'm always missing you

Forever is not always true

I don't want to sound like a bugaboo

But our love was never skewed

Our connection just overgrew

What does she do that I failed too

Lonely:

Living in this pool of regret

I feel like a wreck

My feelings are a threat

My pillow is drenched

No one cares to check

So I stay to the neck

Emotionless:

Don't want your love

Just want your company

You always find a way to comfort me

Sometimes it's nice to just have somebody

Live & learn:

Everyone makes mistakes

You become more awake

But it also makes your heart ache

That dark place,

It's hard to escape

This one's for you:

Can't seem to let go of the memories

Feels like it's been centuries

My heart is in jeopardy

You made me feel carefree

But you left and took my joyous energy

Unfortunate:

Do you ever think about me

We planned to go overseas

Go on shopping sprees

And build our own family tree

Watch yourself:

Emotionally scarred

I got to keep up my guard

Don't want anyone to bombard

Double standards:

I hurt your feelings

And it's a crime

But you hurt mines

And everything is fine

Essential:

I'm at my lowest

I'm feeling hopeless

I'm still broken

But I know the diagnosis

Just needed to start smoking

Gone:

Woke up today feeling sad

Why does heartbreak hurt so bad

You not being here makes me mad

You left me like my deadbeat dad

10 steps back:

Things were starting to get better

I was seeing the brighter side of the weather

But then I began to remember

That you were my treasure

What happen to forever

The lesson:

Pain helped me refocus

Taught me to never be open

Never let my heart get stolen

And appreciate the good moments

Confession:

I still haven't found anyone better

No one has yet to get me wetter

Or match your level of pleasure

I wish you would leave your girl but I don't want you to upset her

All about me:

I am more than my emotion

My intentions are golden

I am very outspoken

It's hard to be open

Just give me an ibuprofen

Since my heart is broken

A fact:

I enjoy the feeling of intimacy

But it causes a lot of difficulty

Hard to tell the level of legitimacy

That you truly feel for me

Falling out:

I don't hear from you at all

When will you call

Did the love fall

Only you can break this wall

Guess I'll just let time heal all

Persistent:

I can be needy

So hard to please me

Understanding me ain't easy

My thoughts make me queasy

And I love too deeply

Overthinking:

Trust issues

Leaving me needing tissues

Mind always in review

Making my feelings renew

Leaving you in the rearview

Nonchalant:

You show no emotion

I'm starting to think you fear devotion

I know your heart feels some commotion

Let me be your life changing potion

Confused:

You said I was immature

I just needed to be reassured

It was the only way to ensure

That your intentions were pure

But you were always obscure

The truth:

I'm not okay

I don't like where I stay

Or how my heart is treated like a stray

I want to runaway

So everything can fade away

Mixed emotions:

Nobody knows how I actually feel

My feelings are sealed

I have a high sex appeal

It's hard to heal

New me:

I am very goal oriented

Emotions can't be fermented

Many have me misrepresented

Feeling discontented

Apart:

We should've stayed friends

In a relationship we could never comprehend

It made us descend

Now we are at an end

Me, myself and I:

Fake friends

A common trend

It's hard to comprehend

All you have is you in the end

Speechless:

You fucked the guy of my dreams

It lowered my self-esteem

It made me scream

Did he make you cream

I thought you were on my team

I guess good girls always find their way downstream

Cheater:

I think you forgot

That you hit the jackpot

Now you're caught

In this love knot

Falling out:

We don't see eye to eye

It makes me cry

Because I just feel the love die

It's time to say goodbye

And let my mind detoxify

Want, desire, lust:

Tired of falling for lames

But who can I blame

Being in a relationship was never his aim

He just liked my brain

But now I'm up on game

Fake love:

I don't really have friends

Most of them came to an end

The love was all pretend

Had to cut them all off to transcend

Fantasy:

I can admit

You really ain't shit

I thought you would commit

But your words were counterfeit

Hopeless romantic:

Told me you were different

But really you were belligerent

I thought you were considerate

But you showed me my feelings weren't significant

Ocean:

Your heart was gold

How did I fold

We were suppose to mold

Guess I didn't have my feelings under control

There were a lot of emotions left untold

Sucks that your heart is already sold

Find a way:

Family is struggling

This time is troubling

I've just been juggling

Might start smuggling

Good mourning:

I try not to dwell

But your name rings a bell

I know you in a nutshell

Sucks that we said our farewells

I still wish you well

A mess:

I'll never forget the disrespect

It made us disconnect

Caused several side effects

I had to redirect

And let my mind reflect

Self-hate:

Always been insecure

Hate what I see in the mirror

Maybe my vision needs to be clearer

So my confidence can appear

Worthless:

Ashamed of my figure

Wish my boobs were bigger

And my skin was clearer

When will I see beauty in the mirror

Hoop:

Tired of the inconsistency

That's the way to get rid of me

I need some efficiency

So your love isn't a mystery

Youngstown:

Your heart is cold

But your soul is gold

You always keep it solid

And let the truth be told

You never let your feelings unfold

You must feel at an absolute threshold

Meaningless:

You're such a mess

You never confess

To the stress that you oppressed

I used to be obsessed

But you no longer impress

Because you only like when I'm undressed

Stay blessed

32:

Didn't want you for your name

I liked how you put me on game

But please don't let your fame

Turn you into a lame

Intimacy:

I miss the feeling of your head between my legs

It made me feel euphoric

Sucks that the feeling is now historic

At least I have it recorded

Deep:

I have many toxic traits that I'm trying to deviate

But my guard acts as a gate

Because no one can relate

To the pain that my heart continuously mutates

I'm my own soulmate

The freak in me:

I can be nasty

And still keep it classy

The thought of you makes me ancy

You make me real splashy

I love it when you talk to me trashy

Do you remember when I was calling you daddy

Crazy story:

You made me feel delusional

The things you did weren't excusable

You were just doing me dirty, as usual

Missing you:

Reminiscing on the good times

When my heart was at its prime

I get sad sometimes

Because I miss my slime

3:21am:

We were suppose to bounce back

What happen to that

I'll always love you

And that's a fact

Repeating cycle:

Standards are high

I'll never find a guy

Most of the time they just drop by

Make me cry

Then leave without saying why

Competitive:

She will never top me

I am the only nominee

Feign:

The thought of you is enticing

Seeing you is exciting

Your kisses are appetizing

I like it when you top me with icing

Rage:

I hate hearing your name

It brings me to flames

And drives me insane

It takes me back to feelings I overcame

Affection:

I did my dirt

Didn't mean to make your heart hurt

Just want you to lose your shirt

And let me be your dessert

Toxic:

Those sneaky link ups only made my feelings come back

You'd eat me up like a snack

Blow out my back

It made me think we were back on track

I keep having drawbacks

The hood in you:

I know you have a hard life

It not hard to recognize

How much you sacrifice

To care for the ones that you prioritize

Your stories make me sympathize

And that dick got me hypnotized

Forgive me:

Haven't talked in so long

I still listen to our song

I hate that I did you wrong

Can we just get along

Butter fingers:

You had the world in your hands

But you still fumbled the bag

I guess you didn't understand

That feelings fade like quicksand

Thief in the night:

Many things can take me off track

But I always find a way to bounce back

Don't want to end up being sidetracked

And get my life hijacked

Money moves:

I enjoy feeling stimulated

But most of the time I get manipulated

Love is overrated

So I'm just money motivated

Because in my mind being broke is terminated

Peace of mind:

Pain makes space for change

You go through more shit as you age

Just burn a little sage

And maybe it'll diminish the rage

There is still hope:

Realigning with my soul

It's just hard to let go

My heart is healing slow

But I'm trying to grow

Another battle:

I learned from my mistakes

They made me break

Then it shaped me like a cake

It seperated my real friends from the fake

Dark times really show who's really here to stay

Never needed nobody:

Nobody to turn to

I have no crew

No one understands what I go through

I'm sorry if I hurt you

You just don't see my point of view

Beyond the surface:

Attaining growth

Need a unique approach

Must keep my feelings close

Can't let anyone impose

Just go with the flow

You'll reach your end goal

Ambivalent:

It feels good to be alive

I just want to thrive

Make it out before I hit twenty-five

And leave toxic people in my archive

Checkmate:

Just tryna get my paper straight

Asked for a lot on my plate

Making room for my growth rate to elevate

My bag is going to be heavyweight

$$$:

I'm tired, but inspired

To be the best version of myself

So that I could reach a high level of wealth

It's important for my health

That there is money stacked under my belt

Beautiful struggle:

Manifesting everything I want

Writing my goals in a bold font

Soon I'll be able to flaunt

All the success that I once sought

Know your worth:

It took me all these years

To get my mind clear

I was ready to disappear

But I overcame the hurt

And had to reassert my worth

11:11

I always been independent

Staying true to myself is my amendment

Growth is my intendment

The process:

Healing is a process

It brings a lot of stress

But as long as you progress

You will reach a level of success

Evolving:

Time to realign.

I've seen all the signs

I always said I was fine,

But deep down inside I was torn and tried to hide

Now I'm just trying to reach my prime

I know I gotta grind

To reach a peace of mind

So I'm just waiting to shine

I will be bigtime

Determined:

I want to be great

I need to accelerate

Migrate to a higher state

So that I can elevate

And the money can perpetuate

My success is what I dictate

Mature:

I use to be a mess

My emotions were a pest

They weren't easy to digest

Then one day I decided it was time to manifest

That decision was the best

Boss:

I'm ambitious

Always knew I was different

My moves are always rigorous

I don't care about all that gibberish

Not with all the ignorance

Don't talk to me if you're illiterate

I only understand people that are deliberate

Relief:

I have to let go

Of anything that doesn't help me grow

Release my emotion like a free throw

And just go with the flow

Guapular:

I have a lot of goals

One is to align with my soul

Take control and get myself out this hole

So that I can make an abundance of bankroll

Reflect:

It's important to reflect

It has a positive affect

It allows you to recollect

And it makes things more direct

Growth:

No longer who I was before

I'm now strong enough to go to war

Got a lot more in store

Opening bigger doors

Definitely ready for more

Outcome:

I'm growing

Soon I'll be glowing

I'm scared of the unknowing

But I just gotta keep going

Content:

I've been feeling so blessed

No longer stressed

Look how much I progressed

I use to be depressed

Heart is finally at rest

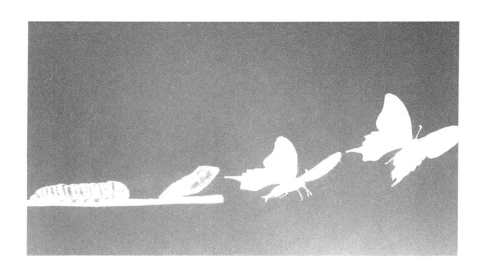

You've made it to the end of the book. I hope it was insightful. It was a reflection of my life and my feelings towards certain situations. There was a lot of built up animosity, sorrow, desire and disappointment, and I was able to release those emotions in this book. I would like to thank you again for supporting my poetry. Those failed relations and disappointing expectations shaped you into who you are today. Always remember that moving on from certain people can draw you closer to your ambitions. Sometimes the absence of certain people gives presence to your blessings. You should always cultivate good thoughts and maintain your energy so that you attract what aligns. Life is about breaking your own limits and outgrowing yourself so that you can reach your fullest potential. Cleanse your soul. Forgive and let go. Be kind. Stay true to yourself. I wish you nothing but positivity, love and happiness.

Love,
Makayla Phomphachanh

CPSIA information can be obtained
at www.ICGtesting.com
Printed in the USA
BVHW030046191020
591161BV00002B/4

9 781984 577429